Life in the Old West

The Wagon Train

Bobbie Kalman

 Crabtree Publishing Company

LIFE IN THE OLD WEST

Created by Bobbie Kalman

In memory of George Abady
(1973-1998)

Editor-in-Chief
Bobbie Kalman

Managing editor
Lynda Hale

Senior editor
April Fast

Project editor
John Crossingham

Research and editing team
Heather Levigne
Kate Calder
Hannelore Sotzek

Photo research
John Crossingham
Hannelore Sotzek

Computer design
Lynda Hale
Robert MacGregor (cover concept)
Campbell Creative Services

Production coordinator
Hannelore Sotzek

Special thanks to
Mary Helmich, California State Parks; Katrina Hoover and Stutter's Fort State Historic Park; Chad Wall, Nebraska State Historical Society; The Church of Jesus Christ of Latter-Day Saints; Janet McMaster, Glenbow Archives; George Robbins

Photographs and reproductions
Albert Bierstadt, Emigrants Crossing the Plains, 1867, National Cowboy Hall of Fame, Oklahoma City: pages 4-5; The Church of Jesus Christ of Latter-Day Saints, Historical Department: page 7 (top); Haymes Foundation Collection, Montana Historical Society / F. Jay Haynes: page 12; Mark Horn: pages 15, 24, 30; The Wheelsoakers ©1982 Tom Lovell, The Greenwich Workshop®, Inc. (detail): pages 28-29; Morning Star Photo/Joseph Stanski: page 10; William Muñoz: page 6; National Museum of American Art, Washington DC/Art Resource, NY (detail): pages 26-27; Nebraska State Historical Society: page 25; Benjamin Reinhart, Emigrant Train Bedding Down for the Night, 1867, from the collection of The Corcoran Gallery of Art, Washington, DC, gift of Mr. and Mrs. Landsell K. Christie: title page (detail), pages 14-15; Tony & Alba Sanches-Zinnanti: page 8 (top); Black Creek Pioneer Village, Toronto (T.R.C.A.): page 8 (bottom); other images by Digital Stock & Image Club Graphics

Illustrations and colorizations
Barbara Bedell: page 13 (bottom)
Bonna Rouse: back cover, pages 6, 11, 16-17, 20-21, 22, 23, 24-25

Crabtree Publishing Company

www.crabtreebooks.com   1-800-387-7650

Printed in Canada/092010/DO20100826

Cataloging in Publication Data
Kalman, Bobbie
  The wagon train
(Life in the Old West)
Includes index.
ISBN 0-7787-0070-4 (library bound) ISBN 0-7787-0102-6 (pbk.) This book descibes the long wagon train journeys to the west—the routes, the wagons, and the daily challenges faced. 1. Pioneers—West (North America)—History—19th century—Juvenile literature. 2. Pioneers—West (North America)—Social life and customs—Juvenile literature. 3. Overland journeys to the Pacific—Juvenile literature. 4. Frontier and pioneer life—West (North America)—Juvenile literature. 5. West (North America)—Social life and customs—Juvenile literature. [1. Overland journeys to the Pacific. 2. Frontier and pioneer life—West (North America)] I. Title. II. Series: Kalman, Bobbie. Life in the Old West.
F596.K358 1999   j978'.02   LC 98-42367
                                                                            CIP

Published in Canada
Crabtree Publishing
616 Welland Ave.
St. Catharines, Ontario
L2M 5V6

Published in the United States
Crabtree Publishing
PMB 59051
350 Fifth Avenue, 59th Floor
New York, New York 10118

Published in the United Kingdom
Crabtree Publishing
Maritime House
Basin Road North, Hove
BN41 1WR

Published in Australia
Crabtree Publishing
386 Mt. Alexander Rd.
Ascot Vale (Melbourne)
VIC 3032

TABLE OF CONTENTS

WAGON TRAINS

Hundreds of years ago, people from Europe began moving to North America. Most of them settled in the eastern United States and in Canada. The west was left unsettled by Europeans for many years. Over time, cities in the east became crowded and busy. Then in the mid-1800s, the American government offered land in the wide-open spaces of the west to anyone who would move there. This land was sold at low prices or even given away!

New land!

People were excited that more land was available for settling. Some people in the east had businesses that were doing poorly, and the west was a place to make a fresh start. Other people wanted to own land for farming. Those who traveled west to begin a new life were called **settlers**, **pioneers**, and **emigrants**.

Safety in numbers

Pioneers packed their belongings and made a long, difficult journey west that lasted up to five months. The travelers faced violent storms, high mountains, wild animals, heat, cold, thirst, starvation, and disease. Families that traveled alone risked death, so most pioneers organized themselves into large groups that provided protection and support on the long journey.

Join the train

The pioneers traveled in **covered wagons**, which carried their belongings. They put a canvas cover on a farm wagon for shelter during the journey. A group of covered wagons traveling together was called a **wagon train**. The wagons moved across the country in a long line, one after the other. If members of one family became ill, other people in the train took care of them. If a wheel broke or fell off a wagon, people from another family pitched in to help fix or replace it. By the mid-1850s, thousands of wagon trains were heading west. These pioneers eventually settled in places such as California, Oregon, Utah, and New Mexico.

Wagon trains in Canada

Wagon trains also existed in Canada in the mid-1800s. Pioneers from eastern Canada traveled west to settle the land around the western forts. Soldiers at these forts needed people to farm the land and produce food for them. Small cities eventually developed around the forts. These cities are now Winnipeg and Edmonton.

The Canadian wagon trains were different from the American ones. The trails in Canada were shorter and followed easier terrain. Traveling by wagon took weeks instead of months. Not many Canadian settlers went west by wagon train, however. Most people traveled west by railway in the late 1800s, when the railroad connecting the east to the west was completed.

Wide rivers and tall mountains were obstacles for a wagon train. Travelers followed trails marked by earlier explorers. The explorers found shallow spots to **ford**, or cross, rivers. They also chose the safest **passes**, or paths, to travel over mountains.

Popular wagon trails

In Canada, the Saskatchewan Trail was an important link between forts in the west. Almost all the westbound trails in the United States began in Independence, Missouri. Thousands of emigrants took these trails. The trails all led to areas that are now some of the biggest cities in western North America.

The wheels of countless wagons dug deep grooves into the prairie soil. Some of these grooves can still be seen today!

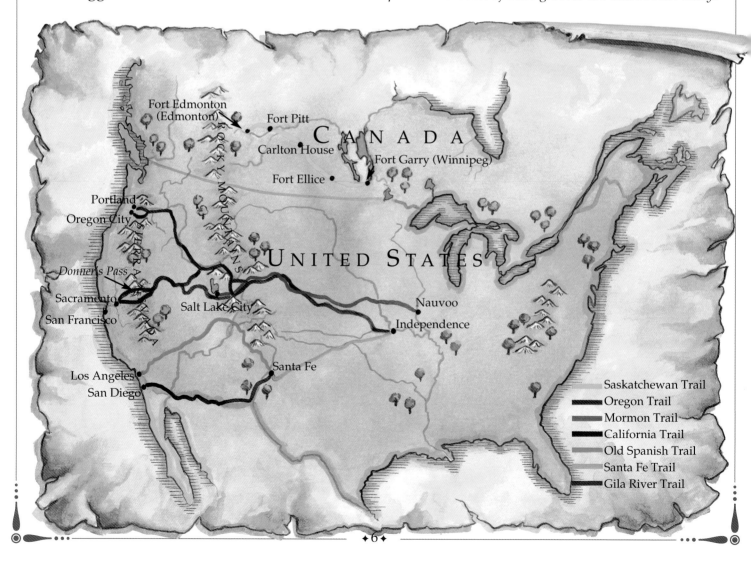

Saskatchewan Trail
Oregon Trail
Mormon Trail
California Trail
Old Spanish Trail
Santa Fe Trail
Gila River Trail

The Mormon Trail

One trail that did not start in Independence was the Mormon Trail. Mormons are members of a religious group who believe they were chosen by God to build a new **Zion**, or holy city. Mormons were often treated badly because of their beliefs, so they needed to find a safe place in which to live and worship. Their leader, Brigham Young, shown in the photograph, selected 144 men to journey west to help find a place for their Zion. Young did not want to take the Oregon Trail because he feared prejudice from pioneers in other wagon trains. He took a different route. The trail started in Nauvoo, Illinois and ended in the Great Salt Valley in Utah. The Mormons made this area their new Zion. This area later became Salt Lake City, shown below.

Pairs of oxen or mules pulled the wagon. They were harnessed together using a yoke. A yoke was a wooden bar with curved pieces that fit around the neck of animals. It was attached to a set of leather or rope reins.

To pioneers on the trail, the covered wagon was home. It carried a family's belongings across the prairie and gave them shelter from harsh weather. A covered wagon was also known as a **prairie schooner**. Schooners are a type of sailboat. From a distance, the wagon's white cover resembled the sail of a ship.

Keep on rolling!

Each wagon had four large wooden wheels. These wheels often broke when traveling over bumpy trails. Supplies were scarce, so sometimes a family's furniture had to be chopped up to make new wheels.

Keeping dry

The cover of the wagon was made of heavy canvas that had been treated with linseed oil. Oil made the cover waterproof. Wooden arches across the top of the wagon supported the cover. If the weather was bad, settlers pulled on ropes called **pucker ropes**. They closed the openings of the cover in the same way you would tighten a hood on a coat. A wagon's cover did more than give shelter. Some settlers sewed pockets onto the cover for extra storage space.

A small space

A wagon was usually 10 feet (3 meters) long and 4 feet (1.2 meters) wide. There was not much space for a family's belongings, which were crammed in tightly. All the items packed on board made the wagon heavy.

Some covered wagons had a bed inside. The bed was placed on top of heavier items in the wagon. A few people slept in the wagon, but there was not enough room for everyone. Most pioneers had to sleep outside in tents.

GETTING READY TO LEAVE

A wagon train was like a tiny, moving town with its own community, food, and tools. Everything from electing a leader to packing a wagon had to be done with care. Although wagon trains passed through a few small towns on the trail, most of their journey took them through the wilderness. Families had to make sure they were prepared for the long trip.

Independence—wagon town!

Independence, Missouri was an important town for travelers on the wagon train. Everything an emigrant needed for the trip could be found in the town. There were trail guides for hire and food, tools, and animals for sale. Wagon shops sold new wagons. Carpenters, blacksmiths, and wheelwrights were available to repair older ones.

The final details

Loading up the wagon was not a pleasant task for the pioneers. They had to make tough choices about what to take. Families argued over what should go into the wagon. Favorite pieces of furniture were left behind to make room for clothes, food, seeds, tools, horseshoes, and guns. Plows, shovels, axes, and a water barrel were strapped to the sides of a wagon.

Pioneers packed their wagons carefully. If they forgot anything, they could not go back for it. Before a wagon train left town, the traveling families held a meeting to set up a **government** for the journey. A captain was elected to lead the way. The group chose other respected individuals to assist the captain in making decisions along the trail.

Get those wagons rolling!

Wagon trains usually left in early May. Everyone was excited on the day of departure. The pioneers could not wait to get to their new land. Leaving town was often slow, however, because people were not used to making such long journeys. Sometimes oxen wandered off or people discovered they had forgotten to pack important tools.

Saying goodbye

Many emigrants left parents, brothers, and sisters behind. The journey west was long and dangerous. The emigrants knew that they might never return. They said a tearful goodbye to friends and relatives and climbed aboard the wagon. One by one, they started down the trail, heading towards their new life.

Timing was important

The wagon trains needed to leave on time because the trails were full of setbacks and dangers that could cause the journey to take longer than planned. Pioneers whose train did not leave on schedule found that the cattle from previous trains had eaten most of the grass, leaving their own cattle with little food.

Other slow-moving wagon trains were caught in fierce mountain blizzards. Delays or disagreements among the travelers also slowed down the trip. It was the captain's job to solve any problems that occurred along the way. He tried his best to move the train along and keep order among the pioneers.

When their wagon was finally packed, pioneer families often posed for a picture.

The captain

The captain was usually a member of one of the families on the train, but sometimes an outsider was hired because he knew the trail well. A captain was also called a **wagon master**. He was responsible for the group and made the important decisions. He chose the date that the train would leave town. The captain also told the train when to move, when to stop, and where to camp at night. He appointed pioneers to guard the camp while everyone else slept. The captain made rules for the people on the wagon train and decided on the punishment if they broke these rules.

HELPFUL ANIMALS

The pioneers brought working animals such as mules, oxen, cattle, and horses with them to make the journey less difficult. Taking care of the animals and keeping them healthy was important. Sometimes pioneers brought their pet dog or cat with them as well.

Herding and hunting

Horses were used to herd the cattle brought along by the pioneers. The cows gave the settlers a source of milk for drinking, cooking, and making butter. Cattle were also an emergency source of food, but pioneers only ate them when there was no other food available. The pioneers hunted game, or wild animals, as often as possible.

Pulling the wagons

Horses were very expensive, and most settlers had only a few. They did not want to tire their horses by having them pull the wagon. Instead, they used mules or oxen.

Mules were strong and quick, but they were stubborn and often stopped in the middle of a trail for no reason. They were also easily spooked. If the pioneers were not careful to tie up their mule, it ran away in the middle of the night!

Slowly, but surely

Oxen were often used to pull wagons because they were reliable. They carried heavier loads than mules, they did not leave the camp, and they were half the price! Oxen were much slower than mules, however. Wagons pulled by oxen sometimes took two weeks longer to arrive than wagons using mules.

The more, the better

At least two oxen or mules were needed to pull a wagon. The animals were very tired by the end of the day. Some families harnessed four, six, or even eight animals to their wagon. These additional animals made the load much lighter to bear. When the load was lighter, the animals remained strong and were able to pull faster.

As the journey wore on, the animals became too tired to pull the wagon. Many settlers had to throw belongings away to make the load lighter for the animals to pull. Pictures, lamps, and heavy furniture were often the first to go.

(left) A mule was easily scared, causing delays, breakdowns, and injuries. Some pioneers attached **blinders** to a mule's harness to block distractions from the animal's view.

(below) The pioneers brought all their animals with them. The horses, oxen, sheep, and dogs rested, ate, and drank when the train stopped for the night. Traveling was hard on the animals, too!

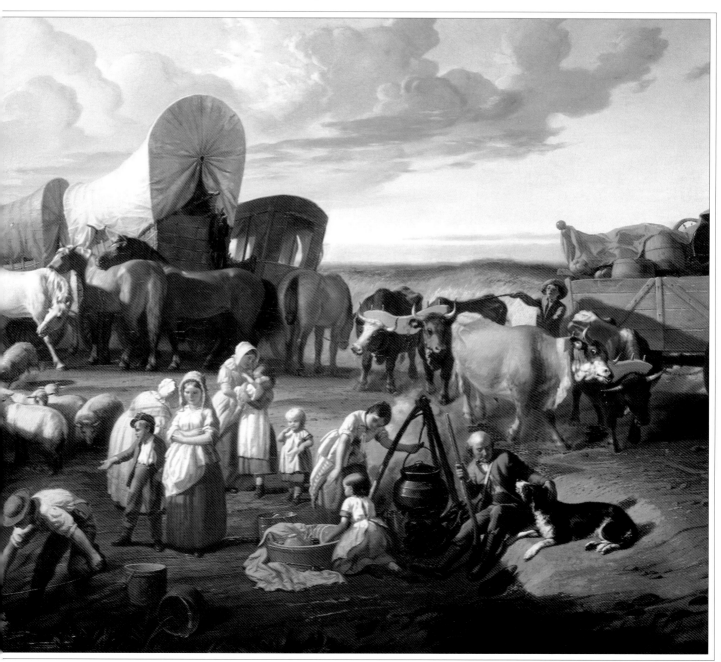

Food and Cooking

Finding game to eat was not always easy. The travelers could go for days on the trail without seeing wild animals to hunt. There was not always enough food to eat. Coming upon a herd of buffalo was reason to celebrate! After a successful hunt, the pioneers feasted on roasted buffalo. They then preserved the leftover meat by drying it over a fire.

Although pioneers hunted for their meat along the trail, they brought other food with them as well. They traveled for months, so their food had to last the whole trip without spoiling. People stocked the wagons with flour, dried fruit, beans, potatoes, and onions. They did not bring fresh fruit or vegetables with them because these foods would not have lasted very long.

Building the fire

Making a good fire was important. A fire was needed to cook the meals and warm the pioneers on cool evenings. The trails had few trees for firewood. Although there was plenty of grass available, it was used only to start fires. The dry prairie grass burned too quickly to make a long-lasting fire. The pioneers gathered **buffalo chips**, or dried buffalo dung, to make a fire that burned for a long time. They stored the buffalo chips under the wagon in a canvas sheet.

Pots and pans

Pioneers had basic utensils for cooking. They boiled water in a kettle. A **skillet**, or pan, and a **dutch oven** were used to cook meat. A dutch oven was a large, deep, metal pot with a lid. Pioneers put food inside it and then placed hot coals underneath the pot and on top of its lid. Heat coming from the top and bottom cooked the food evenly in the dutch oven, just as it does in a regular oven. Pioneers also used the dutch oven for baking.

The menu

The pioneers often had bread, cakes, or biscuits with their meals. Sometimes the dough was mixed with dried fruit to add flavor and nutrients. Meat included deer, buffalo, cattle, and wild birds. Extra meat and leftovers were used to make stew. The fat drippings from meat were mixed with flour to make gravy. In desperate times, pioneers cooked snakes or prairie dogs, but these animals did not taste very good.

Butter made the easy way

Churning butter took a lot of time and effort, so the pioneers found a new way to make it. They hung a bucket of milk at the rear of the wagon. The swaying motion of the wagon shook the milk during the day's journey. By the time the wagon train reached the evening camp, the milk was churned into butter!

After a long day of traveling, the pioneers were tired and hungry. They tethered the horses and oxen so the animals could graze. Settlers then made their camp for the night. They set up tents around the fire and began to prepare their evening meal. Men hunted for fresh meat while women prepared bread and coffee.

Bang! Bang! It was 4 a.m., and the night watchmen had just fired their guns. Julie was still very tired, but it was time to wake up. In three hours the wagon train would be back on the trail, and there was much to do. Julie and her brother Aaron packed away the tent and helped their mother make breakfast.

By sunrise, everyone had started eating. The coffee and biscuits tasted good, but Julie was still hungry. Game had been scarce the last two days. She hoped the hunters would do well today. While their mother put out the fire, Julie and Aaron washed the dishes and packed the kettle and skillet into the wagon. Julie's father put a yoke on the oxen and hitched them to the wagon. They were then ready to leave.

Yesterday, Julie and her family had ridden at the front of the train, so today it was their turn to ride at the rear. The trail was dusty, and she and Aaron kept sneezing, which made their father laugh! To get away from the dust, Julie and Aaron walked through the grass looking for buffalo chips. They talked about what their new home would be like. Some of their friends had already arrived and wrote them letters describing how beautiful the land was. Julie wished they were already there!

Around noon, the wagon train's captain found a good watering hole, so everyone stopped to eat lunch. Julie's father unhitched their oxen so they could graze and get a drink. It was a beautiful day. There were no clouds in the sky, and everywhere Julie looked the land was flat and even. She snacked on buffalo jerky and bread and drank some water. Soon it would be time to leave again.

The afternoon was the worst part of the day. Everyone was tired. The sun was so hot that people just wanted to sleep. Julie steered the wagon while her father talked with Mr. Cole, who was a few wagons ahead. His son Caleb was sick with malaria, and everyone was worried about him. They were concerned that the disease would spread to the rest of the train.

Late in the afternoon the blue sky suddenly grew dark, and Julie heard a deep rumble in the distance. Raindrops began falling like a giant waterfall. "It never rained that hard back home," she thought. People took shelter inside their wagons until the storm broke. When the sun shone through the clouds for the last few hours of the day, the captain called for everyone to set up camp. The wagons moved into a circle, and tents were pitched in the center. Julie and her mother built a fire. The heat warmed her and made her feel better. Just then, Julie's father shouted that the hunters had returned with pheasants for dinner.

Everyone prepared for a long awaited feast! Aaron and his father plucked the feathers off a bird, while Julie and her mother put more buffalo chips on the fire. Julie licked her lips in anticipation of the fresh meat. Jerky was too salty for her tastes. The family members laughed and joked as they cooked and ate.

Julie felt full and satisfied after the delicious meal. She drank a cup of water before she went to bed. Wolves howled in the distance. Julie was so tired that the sounds did not bother her. She fell asleep dreaming of her new home and life in the west. Tomorrow she would be that much closer to the end of their journey!!

The storms in the west were much worse than the ones most pioneers experienced back home. Even the clearest days could end in a late afternoon prairie thunderstorm, which brought high winds, bright lightning, loud thunder, and heavy rain. If the pioneers were lucky, the rain ended by early evening. Often the rain lasted all night long and soaked the wagons and travelers.

Muddy trails

Prairie rain turned dry trails into muddy creeks. Wagon wheels got trapped in the deep mud, and the wagon trains were forced to stop. Pioneers feared that making their animals pull the heavy wagons through mud would tire them. Many captains ordered their trains to wait until the sun dried the trails.

A captain did not stop the train very often, however. It was necessary to move quickly before the winter blizzards started. A blizzard did more damage than any rainstorm!

Deadly snowstorms

Snowy conditions created many obstacles for a wagon train. It was necessary to get through mountains as quickly as possible. The snow could start falling as early as August in the mountainous areas, and blizzards were deadly. Animals could not breathe easily in the thick, blowing snow, causing many of them to die. Wagons would get stuck in the deep snow and stay there for days or weeks. After a blizzard struck, food was hard to find, and fires were difficult to build. Many pioneers ended up starving to death.

The Donner tragedy

In 1846, an Illinois farmer named George Donner organized an 87-person wagon train to ride to Sacramento. They planned to follow the Oregon Trail to the California Trail. The train moved slowly. After reading a trail guidebook, they decided to take a shortcut to the California Trail. The train left the well-used Oregon Trail and was soon in trouble. The shortcut trail needed to be widened, and the wagon train was slowed down even more. It arrived late at the California Trail. Then, after traveling through frigid snowstorms for over a month, the train got stuck in the Sierra mountains in November. There was no game to hunt, and the pioneers had to eat their oxen, mules, and even their pets. The Donner party was rescued in January. By that time, 41 pioneers had died. The path over the mountains where the Donner Train stopped is still called Donner's Pass.

FORDING THE RIVER

The pioneers encountered many rivers, large and small, along the trail. Rivers provided them with water for drinking and for washing their clothes or tools. Rivers had to be forded. Many were shallow and slow, so the wagon trains could ford them by simply driving through.

Panic in the water

Crossing a river was not always easy. The hoofs of the animals could sink into the muddy river bottom, causing oxen and mules to panic and freeze with fear. Pioneers had to urge them along quickly so the wagon would not get stuck. Sometimes when mules crossed a river, they stopped as they reached the shore, but the wagon was still in the river and sank into the mud! Unlucky pioneers with stubborn mules had to dig their wagon out of the mud using spades.

Floating wagons

Sometimes pioneers floated their covered wagons across deep rivers. They filled the seams of the wagons with blankets, mud, or **caulk** to help keep water out. Caulk was a thick, white paste. The pioneers then removed the wagon's wheels and floated the body of the wagon across the river like a small raft. They guided the wagon with poles. The animals crossed by swimming alongside the wagons.

River ferry

As the westward trails became more popular, some people saw a new business opportunity. They set up ferry services to help wagon trains ford the deep rivers. For a fee, workers tied a wagon to a large raft and guided it across to the other shore. Whether the pioneers chose to float their wagon or use the ferry, they had to be careful. Rafts and floating wagons were difficult to control. If the river was moving too quickly, wagon trains had to look for a better spot to ford safely or wait for the water to slow down.

Pioneers often tied a long rope to their wagon when floating it across a river. Someone pulled the rope, while the others in the wagon helped push it along. Everyone had to be careful to keep his or her balance—a family could lose everything if the wagon tipped or sank!

Dangerous Mountains and Deadly Diseases

Mountains and diseases were the two biggest dangers a wagon train had to face. The Rocky and Sierra mountain ranges were deadly places for wagons. The ground was uneven, and steep cliffs and early snowfall made travel difficult. Even without snowstorms, the mountain trails were challenging.

For years, explorers searched the Rockies to find the safest passes for wagons to cross these high mountains. Even the best paths, however, were rocky and bumpy. Some passes were too narrow for the wagons. The pioneers made the trails wider so their wagons could travel on them.

To cross the Rockies, wagon trains had to go up and down many mountain trails. Oxen and mules struggled to get the heavy wagons up bumpy hills. Wagon wheels often broke or got stuck on the large rocks. Some pioneers chipped away rocks with a pickax. Others pushed their wagons up the steep slopes. Once the wagon train finally reached the top of a mountain, everyone had to keep the wagons from rolling out of control on the way down the other side.

Few doctors

Infection and disease were the other major dangers. The west had few doctors, and people did not know how to cure most illnesses. If someone on the train was sick or injured, the pioneers had to be their own doctors. They used books about medicine and healing to learn how to help the sick.

Desperate measures

When someone became ill, people believed that it was "bad blood" that contained the illness. Sick people were often cut to allow the bad blood to flow out. This practice was known as **bloodletting**. Bloodletting made the sick person weak and did not cure them. **Amputation** was another way of dealing with infection. Sometimes, if a settler's arm or leg was badly infected, it was cut off with a saw.

Poor sanitation

The wagon trails were dusty and dirty. Pioneers could not keep their dishes, clothes, or beds clean. Medical tools that were not clean had germs. When these tools were used, they spread germs and caused infections. Lack of proper food made the pioneers too weak to fight infections and diseases.

Quick killers

Once a settler on the wagon train got a disease, it quickly spread to others. Many pioneers died from diseases such as malaria, scurvy, and cholera. Cholera killed settlers so swiftly that people dug a grave for a sick person even before he or she died.

After a few weeks of hard work in the mountains, pioneers were overjoyed to see flat land again. These travelers were tired and hungry, but they were almost home!

NATIVE AMERICANS AND THE WAGON TRAIN

The wagon trains followed many trails that ran through Native American territories. The Native Americans often charged a fee to allow a wagon train to travel across their land. A Native village was a welcome sight to the weary pioneers. The settlers traded with the Native Americans for much-needed food and supplies. The settlers rested briefly near the Native villages.

Losing trust

It was not long, however, before the Native Americans grew to distrust the pioneers, who often treated them with little respect. Pioneers killed off the herds of buffalo on which the Native Americans depended for their survival. When the pioneers hunted buffalo, they took only some parts, leaving the rest of the animal to rot.

Native Americans also hunted buffalo, but they used every part of the animal. They ate the meat and used the hide and bones to make clothing, shelter, and tools. The Native Americans and the buffalo lived in harmony for hundreds of years, but when the pioneers arrived, they killed off the buffalo herds quickly. As the herds disappeared, so did the way of life of the Native Americans.

Bringing sickness

The pioneers did more than just damage the main food and clothing supply of the Native Americans—they also brought new diseases to their villages. Deadly outbreaks of cholera, influenza, typhoid, and smallpox spread quickly. Sometimes a cholera outbreak killed half a village. Soon, many Native Americans wanted nothing to do with the pioneers!

The settlers stopped to soak their wagon wheels in a stream to prevent them from drying and shrinking. Some Native Americans saw the long line of wagons and came to meet the strangers passing through their territory.

Despite many hardships, most pioneers arrived safely at their new land. Families who made the journey with other families now went their separate ways. They bid farewell to friends and began their new lives. They built temporary shacks or tents for shelter. The animals grazed and rested, but the pioneers still had a lot of work to do. The settlers cleared large rocks and trees from their land. They used the wood to build log cabin homes and barns for their animals. They made new furniture to replace the furniture that was lost or destroyed along the journey. It was hard work because they had few tools, but slowly the west became home.

The first winter was difficult for the settlers. Once spring arrived, however, they discovered that their hard work was worthwhile. Oregon had beautiful forests, rich soil, and wild game. The rivers were full of fish. In California, pioneers had warm weather year round. This mild climate was perfect for growing many kinds of fruits and vegetables. The first emigrants who settled these new lands wrote to family and friends in the east to tell them that the west was a great place to live. Wagon trains increased in popularity. By the late 1850s, as many as 55,000 pioneers crossed the country by wagon train each year.

From all around the world

The good word about the North American west spread further than just the east coast. Immigrants from across Europe and Asia boarded ships to America to claim their own piece of the new land. They too made the long, tiring journey to the west. The days of the covered wagon, however, would not last.

From wagon trains to iron trains

By the end of the 1800s, there was a new way to travel west. Railroads were finally built across the United States and Canada. The train, was faster, safer, and more reliable than a covered wagon. A trip that used to take months now took only days. Trains took thousands of people to the west. By the 1900s, wagon trains were a distant memory.

Booming businesses

Soon, western settlements were growing into towns and cities. The emigrants began setting up businesses as more people arrived. Business and trade boomed because of the train. It brought supplies quickly from eastern cities. Western settlers were also able to use the railway to send goods to be sold in the east. The lives of the settlers changed dramatically. They began to enjoy the comforts they had missed. Many settlers became as wealthy or wealthier than those living in the east.

New additions to the west, such as the railroad and telegraph poles, sent buffalo scattering across the plains. Native Americans, who depended on the buffalo for food, were now starving. Their way of life disappeared forever.

Glossary

buffalo chips Dried buffalo dung that was used as fuel for fires

covered wagon A wagon with a canvas top

dutch oven An iron pot used to cook food by placing hot coals beneath it and on its lid

emigrants People who leave their homes to live in another place; also called pioneers or settlers

ford To cross a river

fort A building or group of buildings strong enough to withstand attacks by enemies

government A group of people in charge of making laws for a larger group

immigrants People who come to live in a place that is far from where they were born

jerky Meat that was dried over a fire so that it would not spoil

pass (n) The safest place to travel through mountains or rocky terrain

pioneers People who venture into unsettled areas in order to live there

prairie schooner A covered wagon, which looked like a ship from a distance

prejudice A tendency to treat people unfairly because of their race, religion, or gender

pucker ropes Ropes that could be pulled to close a wagon's cover

settlers People who cleared land and built homes in undeveloped areas

wagon master A wagon-train captain who was hired for his knowledge of the trail

wheelwright A person who makes or repairs wagon wheels

Index